December
Week 52

○ 27. MONDAY

PRIORITIES

○ 28. TUESDAY

○ 29. WEDNESDAY

TO DO

○ 30. THURSDAY

○ 31. FRIDAY

○ 1. SATURDAY / 2. SUNDAY

January

Week 1   01/03/22 - 01/09/22

○ 3. MONDAY

PRIORITIES

○ 4. TUESDAY

○ 5. WEDNESDAY

TO DO

○ 6. THURSDAY

○ 7. FRIDAY

○ 8. SATURDAY / 9. SUNDAY

January

Week 2 01/10/22 - 01/16/22

○ 10. MONDAY

PRIORITIES

○ 11. TUESDAY

○ 12. WEDNESDAY

TO DO

○ 13. THURSDAY

○ 14. FRIDAY

○ 15. SATURDAY / 16. SUNDAY

January

Week 3   01/17/22 - 01/23/22

◯ 17. MONDAY

PRIORITIES

◯ 18. TUESDAY

◯ 19. WEDNESDAY

TO DO

◯ 20. THURSDAY

◯ 21. FRIDAY

◯ 22. SATURDAY / 23. SUNDAY

January

Week 4   01/24/22 - 01/30/22

◯ 24. MONDAY

PRIORITIES

◯ 25. TUESDAY

◯ 26. WEDNESDAY

TO DO

◯ 27. THURSDAY

◯ 28. FRIDAY

◯ 29. SATURDAY / 30. SUNDAY

January

Week 5   01/31/22 - 02/06/22

○ 31. MONDAY

                                          PRIORITIES

○ 1. TUESDAY

○ 2. WEDNESDAY

                                          TO DO

○ 3. THURSDAY

○ 4. FRIDAY

○ 5. SATURDAY / 6. SUNDAY

February

Week 6

02/07/22 - 02/13/22

○ 7. MONDAY

PRIORITIES

○ 8. TUESDAY

○ 9. WEDNESDAY

TO DO

○ 10. THURSDAY

○ 11. FRIDAY

○ 12. SATURDAY / 13. SUNDAY

February

Week 7   02/14/22 - 02/20/22

○ 14. MONDAY

                                              PRIORITIES

○ 15. TUESDAY

○ 16. WEDNESDAY

                                              TO DO

○ 17. THURSDAY

○ 18. FRIDAY

○ 19. SATURDAY / 20. SUNDAY

February

Week 8   02/21/22 - 02/27/22

○ 21. MONDAY

                                          PRIORITIES

○ 22. TUESDAY

○ 23. WEDNESDAY

                                          TO DO

○ 24. THURSDAY

○ 25. FRIDAY

○ 26. SATURDAY / 27. SUNDAY

February

Week 9   02/28/22 - 03/06/22

○ 28. MONDAY

                                          PRIORITIES

○ 1. TUESDAY

○ 2. WEDNESDAY

                                          TO DO

○ 3. THURSDAY

○ 4. FRIDAY

○ 5. SATURDAY / 6. SUNDAY

March

Week 10

03/07/22 - 03/13/22

○ 7. MONDAY

PRIORITIES

○ 8. TUESDAY

○ 9. WEDNESDAY

TO DO

○ 10. THURSDAY

○ 11. FRIDAY

○ 12. SATURDAY / 13. SUNDAY

March

Week 11 — 03/14/22 - 03/20/22

○ 14. MONDAY

PRIORITIES

○ 15. TUESDAY

○ 16. WEDNESDAY

TO DO

○ 17. THURSDAY

○ 18. FRIDAY

○ 19. SATURDAY / 20. SUNDAY

March

Week 12 03/21/22 - 03/27/22

○ 21. MONDAY

PRIORITIES

○ 22. TUESDAY

○ 23. WEDNESDAY

TO DO

○ 24. THURSDAY

○ 25. FRIDAY

○ 26. SATURDAY / 27. SUNDAY

March

Week 13   03/28/22 - 04/03/22

○ 28. MONDAY

PRIORITIES

○ 29. TUESDAY

○ 30. WEDNESDAY

TO DO

○ 31. THURSDAY

○ 1. FRIDAY

○ 2. SATURDAY / 3. SUNDAY

April

Week 14

04/04/22 - 04/10/22

○ 4. MONDAY

PRIORITIES

○ 5. TUESDAY

○ 6. WEDNESDAY

TO DO

○ 7. THURSDAY

○ 8. FRIDAY

○ 9. SATURDAY / 10. SUNDAY

April

Week 15

04/11/22 - 04/17/22

○ 11. MONDAY

PRIORITIES

○ 12. TUESDAY

○ 13. WEDNESDAY

TO DO

○ 14. THURSDAY

○ 15. FRIDAY

○ 16. SATURDAY / 17. SUNDAY

April

Week 16   04/18/22 - 04/24/22

○ 18. MONDAY

                                          PRIORITIES

○ 19. TUESDAY

○ 20. WEDNESDAY

                                          TO DO

○ 21. THURSDAY

○ 22. FRIDAY

○ 23. SATURDAY / 24. SUNDAY

April
Week 17   04/25/22 - 05/01/22

○ 25. MONDAY

                                         PRIORITIES

○ 26. TUESDAY

○ 27. WEDNESDAY

                                         TO DO

○ 28. THURSDAY

○ 29. FRIDAY

○ 30. SATURDAY / 1. SUNDAY

May

Week 18

05/02/22 - 05/08/22

○ 2. MONDAY

PRIORITIES

○ 3. TUESDAY

○ 4. WEDNESDAY

TO DO

○ 5. THURSDAY

○ 6. FRIDAY

○ 7. SATURDAY / 8. SUNDAY

May

Week 19

05/09/22 - 05/15/22

○ 9. MONDAY

PRIORITIES

○ 10. TUESDAY

○ 11. WEDNESDAY

TO DO

○ 12. THURSDAY

○ 13. FRIDAY

○ 14. SATURDAY / 15. SUNDAY

May

Week 20

05/16/22 - 05/22/22

○ 16. MONDAY

PRIORITIES

○ 17. TUESDAY

○ 18. WEDNESDAY

TO DO

○ 19. THURSDAY

○ 20. FRIDAY

○ 21. SATURDAY / 22. SUNDAY

May

Week 21

05/23/22 - 05/29/22

○ 23. MONDAY

PRIORITIES

○ 24. TUESDAY

○ 25. WEDNESDAY

TO DO

○ 26. THURSDAY

○ 27. FRIDAY

○ 28. SATURDAY / 29. SUNDAY

May

Week 22

05/30/22 - 06/05/22

○ 30. MONDAY

PRIORITIES

○ 31. TUESDAY

○ 1. WEDNESDAY

TO DO

○ 2. THURSDAY

○ 3. FRIDAY

○ 4. SATURDAY / 5. SUNDAY

June

Week 23   06/06/22 - 06/12/22

○ 6. MONDAY

PRIORITIES

○ 7. TUESDAY

○ 8. WEDNESDAY

TO DO

○ 9. THURSDAY

○ 10. FRIDAY

○ 11. SATURDAY / 12. SUNDAY

June

Week 24

06/13/22 - 06/19/22

○ 13. MONDAY

PRIORITIES

○ 14. TUESDAY

○ 15. WEDNESDAY

TO DO

○ 16. THURSDAY

○ 17. FRIDAY

○ 18. SATURDAY / 19. SUNDAY

June

Week 25

06/20/22 - 06/26/22

○ 20. MONDAY

PRIORITIES

○ 21. TUESDAY

○ 22. WEDNESDAY

TO DO

○ 23. THURSDAY

○ 24. FRIDAY

○ 25. SATURDAY / 26. SUNDAY

June

Week 26

06/27/22 - 07/03/22

○ 27. MONDAY

PRIORITIES

○ 28. TUESDAY

○ 29. WEDNESDAY

TO DO

○ 30. THURSDAY

○ 1. FRIDAY

○ 2. SATURDAY / 3. SUNDAY

July
Week 27

07/04/22 - 07/10/22

○ 4. MONDAY

PRIORITIES

○ 5. TUESDAY

○ 6. WEDNESDAY

TO DO

○ 7. THURSDAY

○ 8. FRIDAY

○ 9. SATURDAY / 10. SUNDAY

July
Week 28

07/11/22 - 07/17/22

○ 11. MONDAY

PRIORITIES

○ 12. TUESDAY

○ 13. WEDNESDAY

TO DO

○ 14. THURSDAY

○ 15. FRIDAY

○ 16. SATURDAY / 17. SUNDAY

July
Week 29

07/18/22 - 07/24/22

○ 18. MONDAY

PRIORITIES

○ 19. TUESDAY

○ 20. WEDNESDAY

TO DO

○ 21. THURSDAY

○ 22. FRIDAY

○ 23. SATURDAY / 24. SUNDAY

July
Week 30   07/25/22 - 07/31/22

○ 25. MONDAY

                                           PRIORITIES

○ 26. TUESDAY

○ 27. WEDNESDAY

                                           TO DO

○ 28. THURSDAY

○ 29. FRIDAY

○ 30. SATURDAY / 31. SUNDAY

August

Week 31   08/01/22 - 08/07/22

○ 1. MONDAY

　　　　　　　　　　　　　　　　　　　PRIORITIES

○ 2. TUESDAY

○ 3. WEDNESDAY

　　　　　　　　　　　　　　　　　　　TO DO

○ 4. THURSDAY

○ 5. FRIDAY

○ 6. SATURDAY / 7. SUNDAY

August

Week 32

08/08/22 - 08/14/22

○ 8. MONDAY

PRIORITIES

○ 9. TUESDAY

○ 10. WEDNESDAY

TO DO

○ 11. THURSDAY

○ 12. FRIDAY

○ 13. SATURDAY / 14. SUNDAY

August

Week 33   08/15/22 - 08/21/22

○ 15. MONDAY

                                               PRIORITIES

○ 16. TUESDAY

○ 17. WEDNESDAY

                                               TO DO

○ 18. THURSDAY

○ 19. FRIDAY

○ 20. SATURDAY / 21. SUNDAY

August

Week 34   08/22/22 - 08/28/22

○ 22. MONDAY

                                               PRIORITIES

○ 23. TUESDAY

○ 24. WEDNESDAY

                                               TO DO

○ 25. THURSDAY

○ 26. FRIDAY

○ 27. SATURDAY / 28. SUNDAY

August

Week 35

08/29/22 - 09/04/22

○ 29. MONDAY

PRIORITIES

○ 30. TUESDAY

○ 31. WEDNESDAY

TO DO

○ 1. THURSDAY

○ 2. FRIDAY

○ 3. SATURDAY / 4. SUNDAY

September

Week 36   09/05/22 - 09/11/22

○ 5. MONDAY

PRIORITIES

○ 6. TUESDAY

○ 7. WEDNESDAY

TO DO

○ 8. THURSDAY

○ 9. FRIDAY

○ 10. SATURDAY / 11. SUNDAY

September

Week 37   09/12/22 - 09/18/22

○ 12. MONDAY

                                                      PRIORITIES

○ 13. TUESDAY

○ 14. WEDNESDAY

                                                      TO DO

○ 15. THURSDAY

○ 16. FRIDAY

○ 17. SATURDAY / 18. SUNDAY

September

Week 38

09/19/22 - 09/25/22

○ 19. MONDAY

PRIORITIES

○ 20. TUESDAY

○ 21. WEDNESDAY

TO DO

○ 22. THURSDAY

○ 23. FRIDAY

○ 24. SATURDAY / 25. SUNDAY

September

Week 39   09/26/22 - 10/02/22

○ 26. MONDAY

PRIORITIES

○ 27. TUESDAY

○ 28. WEDNESDAY

TO DO

○ 29. THURSDAY

○ 30. FRIDAY

○ 1. SATURDAY / 2. SUNDAY

October

Week 40

10/03/22 - 10/09/22

○ 3. MONDAY

PRIORITIES

○ 4. TUESDAY

○ 5. WEDNESDAY

TO DO

○ 6. THURSDAY

○ 7. FRIDAY

○ 8. SATURDAY / 9. SUNDAY

October

Week 41   10/10/22 - 10/16/22

○ 10. MONDAY

PRIORITIES

○ 11. TUESDAY

○ 12. WEDNESDAY

TO DO

○ 13. THURSDAY

○ 14. FRIDAY

○ 15. SATURDAY / 16. SUNDAY

October

Week 42   10/17/22 - 10/23/22

○ 17. MONDAY

                                             PRIORITIES

○ 18. TUESDAY

○ 19. WEDNESDAY

                                             TO DO

○ 20. THURSDAY

○ 21. FRIDAY

○ 22. SATURDAY / 23. SUNDAY

October

Week 43   10/24/22 - 10/30/22

○ 24. MONDAY

                           PRIORITIES

○ 25. TUESDAY

○ 26. WEDNESDAY

                           TO DO

○ 27. THURSDAY

○ 28. FRIDAY

○ 29. SATURDAY / 30. SUNDAY

October

Week 44					10/31/22 - 11/06/22

○ 31. MONDAY

PRIORITIES

○ 1. TUESDAY

○ 2. WEDNESDAY

TO DO

○ 3. THURSDAY

○ 4. FRIDAY

○ 5. SATURDAY / 6. SUNDAY

November

Week 45 11/07/22 - 11/13/22

◯ 7. MONDAY

PRIORITIES

◯ 8. TUESDAY

◯ 9. WEDNESDAY

TO DO

◯ 10. THURSDAY

◯ 11. FRIDAY

◯ 12. SATURDAY / 13. SUNDAY

November

Week 46   11/14/22 - 11/20/22

○ 14. MONDAY

                                         PRIORITIES

○ 15. TUESDAY

○ 16. WEDNESDAY

                                         TO DO

○ 17. THURSDAY

○ 18. FRIDAY

○ 19. SATURDAY / 20. SUNDAY

November

Week 47   11/21/22 - 11/27/22

○ **21. MONDAY**

                                                                PRIORITIES

○ **22. TUESDAY**

○ **23. WEDNESDAY**

                                                                TO DO

○ **24. THURSDAY**

○ **25. FRIDAY**

○ **26. SATURDAY / 27. SUNDAY**

November

Week 48

11/28/22 - 12/04/22

○ 28. MONDAY

PRIORITIES

○ 29. TUESDAY

○ 30. WEDNESDAY

TO DO

○ 1. THURSDAY

○ 2. FRIDAY

○ 3. SATURDAY / 4. SUNDAY

December

Week 49   12/05/22 - 12/11/22

○ 5. MONDAY

PRIORITIES

○ 6. TUESDAY

○ 7. WEDNESDAY

TO DO

○ 8. THURSDAY

○ 9. FRIDAY

○ 10. SATURDAY / 11. SUNDAY

December

Week 50

12/12/22 - 12/18/22

○ 12. MONDAY

PRIORITIES

○ 13. TUESDAY

○ 14. WEDNESDAY

TO DO

○ 15. THURSDAY

○ 16. FRIDAY

○ 17. SATURDAY / 18. SUNDAY

December

Week 51   12/19/22 - 12/25/22

○ 19. MONDAY

                                                  PRIORITIES

○ 20. TUESDAY

○ 21. WEDNESDAY

                                                  TO DO

○ 22. THURSDAY

○ 23. FRIDAY

○ 24. SATURDAY / 25. SUNDAY

December

Week 52

12/26/22 - 01/01/23

○ 26. MONDAY

PRIORITIES

○ 27. TUESDAY

○ 28. WEDNESDAY

TO DO

○ 29. THURSDAY

○ 30. FRIDAY

○ 31. SATURDAY / 1. SUNDAY

January

Week 1   01/02/23 - 01/08/23

○ 2. MONDAY

PRIORITIES

○ 3. TUESDAY

○ 4. WEDNESDAY

TO DO

○ 5. THURSDAY

○ 6. FRIDAY

○ 7. SATURDAY / 8. SUNDAY

January

Week 2   01/09/23 - 01/15/23

○ 9. MONDAY

                                                PRIORITIES

○ 10. TUESDAY

○ 11. WEDNESDAY

                                                TO DO

○ 12. THURSDAY

○ 13. FRIDAY

○ 14. SATURDAY / 15. SUNDAY

January

Week 3					01/16/23 - 01/22/23

○ 16. MONDAY

PRIORITIES

○ 17. TUESDAY

○ 18. WEDNESDAY

TO DO

○ 19. THURSDAY

○ 20. FRIDAY

○ 21. SATURDAY / 22. SUNDAY

January

Week 4

01/23/23 - 01/29/23

◯ 23. MONDAY

PRIORITIES

◯ 24. TUESDAY

◯ 25. WEDNESDAY

TO DO

◯ 26. THURSDAY

◯ 27. FRIDAY

◯ 28. SATURDAY / 29. SUNDAY

January

Week 5   01/30/23 - 02/05/23

○ 30. MONDAY

                                                PRIORITIES

○ 31. TUESDAY

○ 1. WEDNESDAY

                                                TO DO

○ 2. THURSDAY

○ 3. FRIDAY

○ 4. SATURDAY / 5. SUNDAY

February

Week 6

02/06/23 - 02/12/23

○ 6. MONDAY

PRIORITIES

○ 7. TUESDAY

○ 8. WEDNESDAY

TO DO

○ 9. THURSDAY

○ 10. FRIDAY

○ 11. SATURDAY / 12. SUNDAY

February

Week 7   02/13/23 - 02/19/23

○ 13. MONDAY

                                              PRIORITIES

○ 14. TUESDAY

○ 15. WEDNESDAY

                                              TO DO

○ 16. THURSDAY

○ 17. FRIDAY

○ 18. SATURDAY / 19. SUNDAY

February

Week 8   02/20/23 - 02/26/23

○ 20. MONDAY

                                         PRIORITIES

○ 21. TUESDAY

○ 22. WEDNESDAY

                                         TO DO

○ 23. THURSDAY

○ 24. FRIDAY

○ 25. SATURDAY / 26. SUNDAY

February

Week 9   02/27/23 - 03/05/23

○ 27. MONDAY

PRIORITIES

○ 28. TUESDAY

○ 1. WEDNESDAY

TO DO

○ 2. THURSDAY

○ 3. FRIDAY

○ 4. SATURDAY / 5. SUNDAY

March

Week 10

03/06/23 - 03/12/23

○ 6. MONDAY

PRIORITIES

○ 7. TUESDAY

○ 8. WEDNESDAY

TO DO

○ 9. THURSDAY

○ 10. FRIDAY

○ 11. SATURDAY / 12. SUNDAY

March

Week 11											03/13/23 - 03/19/23

○ 13. MONDAY

PRIORITIES

○ 14. TUESDAY

○ 15. WEDNESDAY

TO DO

○ 16. THURSDAY

○ 17. FRIDAY

○ 18. SATURDAY / 19. SUNDAY

March

Week 12

03/20/23 - 03/26/23

○ 20. MONDAY

PRIORITIES

○ 21. TUESDAY

○ 22. WEDNESDAY

TO DO

○ 23. THURSDAY

○ 24. FRIDAY

○ 25. SATURDAY / 26. SUNDAY

March

Week 13   03/27/23 - 04/02/23

○ 27. MONDAY

                                           PRIORITIES

○ 28. TUESDAY

○ 29. WEDNESDAY

                                           TO DO

○ 30. THURSDAY

○ 31. FRIDAY

○ 1. SATURDAY / 2. SUNDAY

April

Week 14   04/03/23 - 04/09/23

○ 3. MONDAY

                                                       PRIORITIES

○ 4. TUESDAY

○ 5. WEDNESDAY

                                                       TO DO

○ 6. THURSDAY

○ 7. FRIDAY

○ 8. SATURDAY / 9. SUNDAY

April

Week 15

04/10/23 - 04/16/23

○ 10. MONDAY

PRIORITIES

○ 11. TUESDAY

○ 12. WEDNESDAY

TO DO

○ 13. THURSDAY

○ 14. FRIDAY

○ 15. SATURDAY / 16. SUNDAY

April

Week 16

04/17/23 - 04/23/23

○ 17. MONDAY

PRIORITIES

○ 18. TUESDAY

○ 19. WEDNESDAY

TO DO

○ 20. THURSDAY

○ 21. FRIDAY

○ 22. SATURDAY / 23. SUNDAY

April

Week 17

04/24/23 - 04/30/23

○ 24. MONDAY

PRIORITIES

○ 25. TUESDAY

○ 26. WEDNESDAY

TO DO

○ 27. THURSDAY

○ 28. FRIDAY

○ 29. SATURDAY / 30. SUNDAY

May

Week 18

05/01/23 - 05/07/23

○ 1. MONDAY

PRIORITIES

○ 2. TUESDAY

○ 3. WEDNESDAY

TO DO

○ 4. THURSDAY

○ 5. FRIDAY

○ 6. SATURDAY / 7. SUNDAY

May

Week 19

05/08/23 - 05/14/23

○ 8. MONDAY

PRIORITIES

○ 9. TUESDAY

○ 10. WEDNESDAY

TO DO

○ 11. THURSDAY

○ 12. FRIDAY

○ 13. SATURDAY / 14. SUNDAY

May
Week 20

05/15/23 - 05/21/23

○ 15. MONDAY

PRIORITIES

○ 16. TUESDAY

○ 17. WEDNESDAY

TO DO

○ 18. THURSDAY

○ 19. FRIDAY

○ 20. SATURDAY / 21. SUNDAY

May

Week 21   05/22/23 - 05/28/23

○ 22. MONDAY

PRIORITIES

○ 23. TUESDAY

○ 24. WEDNESDAY

TO DO

○ 25. THURSDAY

○ 26. FRIDAY

○ 27. SATURDAY / 28. SUNDAY

May

Week 22

05/29/23 - 06/04/23

○ 29. MONDAY

PRIORITIES

○ 30. TUESDAY

○ 31. WEDNESDAY

TO DO

○ 1. THURSDAY

○ 2. FRIDAY

○ 3. SATURDAY / 4. SUNDAY

June

Week 23

06/05/23 - 06/11/23

○ 5. MONDAY

PRIORITIES

○ 6. TUESDAY

○ 7. WEDNESDAY

TO DO

○ 8. THURSDAY

○ 9. FRIDAY

○ 10. SATURDAY / 11. SUNDAY

June

Week 24   06/12/23 - 06/18/23

○ 12. MONDAY

                                           PRIORITIES

○ 13. TUESDAY

○ 14. WEDNESDAY

                                           TO DO

○ 15. THURSDAY

○ 16. FRIDAY

○ 17. SATURDAY / 18. SUNDAY

June

Week 25

06/19/23 - 06/25/23

○ 19. MONDAY

PRIORITIES

○ 20. TUESDAY

○ 21. WEDNESDAY

TO DO

○ 22. THURSDAY

○ 23. FRIDAY

○ 24. SATURDAY / 25. SUNDAY

June

Week 26   06/26/23 - 07/02/23

○ 26. MONDAY

PRIORITIES

○ 27. TUESDAY

○ 28. WEDNESDAY

TO DO

○ 29. THURSDAY

○ 30. FRIDAY

○ 1. SATURDAY / 2. SUNDAY

Made in the USA
Monee, IL
27 December 2022

23696696R00044